THE DECLARATION OF THE RIGHTS OF MAN AND OF CITIZENS

A Contribution to Modern Constitutional History

BY

GEORG JELLINEK, Dr. Phil. et Jur.
Professor of Law in the University of Heidelberg

AUTHORIZED TRANSLATION FROM THE GERMAN

BY

MAX FARRAND, Ph.D.
Professor of History in Wesleyan University

REVISED BY THE AUTHOR

NEW YORK
HENRY HOLT AND COMPANY

Copyright, 1901,
BY
HENRY HOLT & CO.

JC
571
J413
1901

ROBERT DRUMMOND, PRINTER, NEW YORK.

TRANSLATOR'S PREFACE.

ALTHOUGH several years have elapsed since this essay was published, it has apparently come to the attention of only a few specialists, and those almost exclusively in modern European history. It deserves consideration by all students of history, and it is of special importance to those who are interested in the early constitutional history of the United States, for it traces the origin of the enactment of bills of rights. In the hope that it will be brought before a larger number of students who realize the significance of this question and who appreciate genuine scholarly work, this essay is now translated.

M. F.

WESLEYAN UNIVERSITY,
   MIDDLETOWN, CT., March 1, 1901.

PREFACE.

THE following essay has originated in connection with a larger work upon which I have been engaged for some time. May it assist in strengthening the conviction that the ideas expressed in the law of the modern state are to be comprehended not alone through the history of the literature and the development of the conceptions of right, but above all through that history of the institutions themselves that stretches itself over the whole field of our civilized life!

G. J.

HEIDELBERG, June 23, 1895.

TABLE OF CONTENTS.

CHAPTER PAGE
I. THE FRENCH DECLARATION OF RIGHTS OF AUGUST 26, 1789, AND ITS SIGNIFICANCE 1
II. ROUSSEAU'S "CONTRAT SOCIAL" WAS NOT THE SOURCE OF THIS DECLARATION.... 8
III. THE BILLS OF RIGHTS OF THE INDIVIDUAL STATES OF THE NORTH AMERICAN UNION WERE ITS MODELS............ 13
IV. VIRGINIA'S BILL OF RIGHTS AND THOSE OF THE OTHER NORTH AMERICAN STATES. 22
V. COMPARISON OF THE FRENCH AND AMERICAN DECLARATIONS................. 27
VI. THE CONTRAST BETWEEN THE AMERICAN AND ENGLISH DECLARATIONS OF RIGHTS 43
VII. RELIGIOUS LIBERTY IN THE ANGLO-AMERICAN COLONIES THE SOURCE OF THE IDEA OF ESTABLISHING BY LAW A UNIVERSAL RIGHT OF MAN..................... 59
VIII. THE CREATION OF A SYSTEM OF RIGHTS OF MAN AND OF CITIZENS DURING THE AMERICAN REVOLUTION.............. 78
IX. THE RIGHTS OF MAN AND THE TEUTONIC CONCEPTION OF RIGHT............... 90

THE DECLARATION OF THE RIGHTS OF MAN AND OF CITIZENS.

CHAPTER I.

THE FRENCH DECLARATION OF RIGHTS OF AUGUST 26, 1789, AND ITS SIGNIFICANCE.

THE declaration of "the rights of man and of citizens" by the French Constituent Assembly on August 26, 1789, is one of the most significant events of the French Revolution. It has been criticised from different points of view with directly opposing results. The political scientist and the historian, thoroughly appreciating its importance, have repeatedly come to the conclusion that the Declaration had no small part in the anarchy with which France was visited soon after the storming of the Bastille. They point to its abstract phrases as ambiguous and therefore dangerous, and as void of all political reality and practical statesmanship. Its empty pathos, they say, confused the mind, disturbed calm judgment, aroused passions, and stifled the sense of duty,—for of duty there is not a word.[1] Others, on the contrary, and especially Frenchmen, have exalted it as a revelation in the world's history, as a catechism of the "principles of 1789" which form the eternal foundation of the state's structure, and they have glorified it as the most precious gift that France has given to mankind.

Less regarded than its historical and political significance is the importance of this document in the history of law, an importance which continues even to the present day. Whatever may be the value or worthlessness of its general phrases, it is under the influence of this document that the conception of the public rights of the individual has developed in the positive law of the states of the European continent. Until it appeared

[1] First of all, as is well known, Burke and Bentham, and later Taine, *Les origines de la France contemporaine: La révolution*, I, pp. 273 *et seq.;* Oncken, *Das Zeitalter der Revolution, des Kaiserreiches und der Befreiungskriege*, I, pp. 229 *et seq.;* and Weiss, *Geschichte der französischen Revolution*, 1888, I, p. 263.

public law literature recognized the rights of heads of states, the privileges of class, and the privileges of individuals or special corporations, but the general rights of subjects were to be found essentially only in the form of duties on the part of the state, not in the form of definite legal claims of the individual. The Declaration of the Rights of Man for the first time originated in all its vigor in positive law the conception, which until then had been known only to natural law, of the personal rights of the members of the state over against the state as a whole. This was next seen in the first French constitution of September 3, 1791, which set forth, upon the basis of a preceding declaration of rights, a list of *droits naturels et civils* as rights that were guaranteed by the constitution.[2] Together with the right of suffrage, the "*droits garantis par la constitution*", which were enumerated for the last time in the constitution of November 4, 1848,[3] form to-day the basis of French theory and practice respecting the personal public rights of the indi-

[2] Titre premier: "Dispositions fondamentales garanties par la constitution."

[3] Hélie, *Les constitutions de la France*, pp. 1103 *et seq.*

vidual.[4] And under the influence of the French declaration there have been introduced into almost all of the constitutions of the other Continental states similar enumerations of rights, whose separate phrases and formulas, however, are more or less adapted to the particular conditions of their respective states, and therefore frequently exhibit wide differences in content.

In Germany most of the constitutions of the period prior to 1848 contained a section upon the rights of subjects, and in the year 1848 the National Constitutional Convention at Frankfort adopted "the fundamental rights of the German people", which were published on December 27, 1848, as Federal law. In spite of a resolution of the *Bund* of August 23, 1851, declaring these rights null and void, they are of lasting importance, because many of their specifications are to-day incorporated almost word for word in the existing Federal law.[5] These enumerations of rights appear in greater numbers in

---

[4] *Cf.* Jellinek, *System der subjektiven öffentlichen Rechte*, p. 3, n. 1.

[5] Binding, *Der Versuch der Reichsgründung durch die Paulskirche*, Leipzig, 1892, p. 23.

the European constitutions of the period after 1848. Thus, first of all, in the Prussian constitution of January 31, 1850, and in Austria's "Fundamental Law of the State" of December 21, 1867, on the general rights of the state's citizens. And more recently they have been incorporated in the constitutions of the new states in the Balkan peninsula.

A noteworthy exception to this are the constitutions of the North German Confederation of July 26, 1867, and of the German Empire of April 16, 1871, which lack entirely any paragraph on fundamental rights. The constitution of the Empire, however, could the better dispense with such a declaration as it was already contained in most of the constitutions of the individual states, and, as above stated, a series of Federal laws has enacted the most important principles of the Frankfort fundamental rights. Besides, with the provisions of the Federal constitution as to amendments, it was not necessary to make any special place for them in that instrument, as the Reichstag, to whose especial care the guardianship of the fundamental rights must be entrusted, has no difficult forms to observe in amending the constitution.⁶ As a matter of fact the public rights of the individual are much greater in the German Empire than in most of the states where the fundamental rights are specifically set forth in the constitution. This may be seen, for example, by a glance at the legislation and the judicial and administrative practice in Austria.

But whatever may be one's opinion to-day upon the formulation of abstract principles, which only become vitalized through the process of detailed legislation, as affecting the legal position of the individual in the state, the fact that the recognition of such principles is historically bound up with that first declaration of rights makes it an important task of constitutional history to ascertain the origin of the French Declaration of Rights of 1789. The achievement of this task is of great importance both in explaining the development of the modern state and in understanding the position which this state assures to the individual. Thus

⁶ When considering the constitution, the Reichstag rejected all proposals which aimed to introduce fundamental rights. *Cf.* Bezold, *Materialen der deutschen Reichsverfassung*, III, pp. 896–1010.

OF THE RIGHTS OF MAN. 7

far in the works on public law various precursors of the declaration of the Constituent Assembly, from Magna Charta to the American Declaration of Independence, have been enumerated and arranged in regular sequence, yet any thorough investigation of the sources from which the French drew is not to be found.

It is the prevailing opinion that the teachings of the *Contrat Social* gave the impulse to the Declaration, and that its prototype was the Declaration of Independence of the thirteen United States of North America. Let us first of all inquire into the correctness of these assumptions.

CHAPTER II.

ROUSSEAU'S *CONTRAT SOCIAL* WAS NOT THE SOURCE OF THIS DECLARATION.

IN his *History of Political Science*—the most comprehensive work of that kind which France possesses — Paul Janet, after a thorough presentation of the *Contrat Social*, discusses the influence which this work of Rousseau's exercised upon the Revolution. The idea of the declaration of rights is to be traced back to Rousseau's teachings. What else is the declaration itself than the formulation of the state contract according to Rousseau's ideas? And what are the several rights but the stipulations and specifications of that contract?[1]

---

[1] " Est-il nécessaire de prouver, qu'un tel acte ne vient point de Montesquieu, mais de J.-J. Rousseau? . . . Mais l'acte même de la déclaration est-il autre chose que le contrat passé entre tous les membres de la communauté, selon les

It is hard to understand how an authority upon the *Contrat Social* could make such a statement though in accord with popular opinion.

The social contract has only one stipulation, namely, the complete transference to the community of all the individual's rights.[2] The individual does not retain one particle of his rights from the moment he enters the state.[3] Everything that he receives of the nature of right he gets from the *volonté générale*, which is the sole judge of its own limits, and ought not to be, and cannot be, restricted by the law of any power. Even property belongs to the individual only by virtue of state concession. The social contract makes the state the master of the goods

---

idées de Rousseau ? N'est ce pas l'énonciation des clauses et des conditions de ce contrat ?"— *Histoire de la science politique, 3me éd.*, pp. 457, 458.

[2] "Ces clauses, bien entendues, se réduisent toutes à une seule: savoir, l'aliénation totale de chaque associé avec tous ses droits à toute la communauté."—*Du contrat social*, I, 6.

[3] "De plus, l'aliénation se faisant sans réserve, l'union est aussi parfaite qu'elle peut l'être et nul associé n'a plus rien à réclamer." I, 6.

of its members,[4] and the latter remain in possession only as the trustees of public property.[5] Civil liberty consists simply of what is left to the individual after taking his duties as a citizen into account.[6] These duties can only be imposed by law, and according to the social contract the laws must be the same for all citizens. This is the only restriction upon the sovereign power,[7] but it is a restriction which follows from the very nature of that power, and it carries in itself its own guarantees.[8]

[4] "Car l'État, à l'égard de ses membres, est maître de tous leurs biens par le contrat social." I, 9.

[5] ". . . Les possesseurs étant considérés comme dépositaires du bien public." I, 9.

[6] "On convient que tout ce que chacun aliène, par le pacte social, de sa puissance, de ses biens, de sa liberté, c'est seulement la partie de tout cela dont l'usage importe à la communauté; mais il faut convenir aussi que le souverain seul est juge de cette importance." II, 4.

[7] "Ainsi, par la nature du pacte, tout acte de souveraineté, c'est-à-dire toute acte authentique de la volonté générale, oblige ou favorise également tous les citoyens." II, 4.

[8] "La puissance souveraine n'a nul besoin de garant envers les sujets." I, 7.

The conception of an original right, which man brings with him into society and which appears as a restriction upon the rights of the sovereign, is specifically rejected by Rousseau. There is no fundamental law which can be binding upon the whole people, not even the social contract itself.[9]

The Declaration of Rights, however, would draw dividing lines between the state and the individual, which the lawmaker should ever keep before his eyes as the limits that have been set him once and for all by "the natural, inalienable and sacred rights of man."[10]

The principles of the *Contrat Social* are accordingly at enmity with every declaration of rights. For from these principles there

[9] " Il est contre la nature du corps politique que le souverain s'impose une loi qu'il ne puisse enfreindre . . . il n'y a ni ne peut y avoir nulle espèce de loi fundamentale obligatoire pour le corps du peuple, pas même le contrat social." I, 7.

[10] Constitution du 3 septembre 1791, titre premier: "Le pouvoir législatif ne pourra faire aucune loi qui porte atteinte et mette obstacle à l'exercise de droits naturels et civils consignés dans le présent titre, et garantis par la constitution."

ensues not the right of the individual, but the omnipotence of the common will, unrestricted by law. Taine comprehended better than Janet the consequences of the *Contrat Social.*[11]

The Declaration of August 26, 1789, originated in opposition to the *Contrat Social.* The ideas of the latter work exercised, indeed, a certain influence upon the style of some clauses of the Declaration, but the conception of the Declaration itself must have come from some other source.

[11] *Cf.* Taine, *loc. cit.: L'ancien régime*, pp. 321 *et seq.*

CHAPTER III.

THE BILLS OF RIGHTS OF THE INDIVIDUAL STATES OF THE NORTH AMERICAN UNION WERE ITS MODELS.

THE conception of a declaration of rights had found expression in France even before the assembling of the States General. It had already appeared in a number of *cahiers*. The *cahier* of the *Bailliage* of Nemours is well worth noting, as it contained a chapter entitled "On the Necessity of a Declaration of the Rights of Man and of Citizens",[1] and sketched a plan of such a declaration with thirty articles. Among other plans that in the *cahier des tiers état* of the city of Paris has some interest.[2]

[1] " De la nécessité d'établir quels sont les droits de l'homme et des citoyens, et d'en faire une déclaration qu'ils puissent opposer à toutes les espèces d'injustice."—*Archives parlementaires I. Série*, IV, pp. 161 *et seq.*

[2] *Archives parl.*, V, pp. 281 *et seq.*

In the National Assembly, however, it was Lafayette who on July 11, 1789, made the motion to enact a declaration of rights in connection with the constitution, and he therewith laid before the assembly a plan of such a declaration.[3]

It is the prevailing opinion that Lafayette was inspired to make this motion by the North American Declaration of Independence.[4] And this instrument is further declared to have been the model that the Constituent Assembly had in mind in framing its declaration. The sharp, pointed style and the practical character of the American document are cited by many as in praiseworthy contrast to the confusing verbosity and dogmatic theory of the French Declaration.[5] Others bring forward, as a

[3] *Arch. parl.*, VIII, pp. 221, 222.

[4] *Cf. e.g.* H. v. Sybel, *Geschichte der Revolutionszeit von 1789 bis 1800*, 4. Aufl., I, p. 73.

[5] *Cf.* Häusser, *Geschichte der franz. Revolution*, 3. Aufl., p. 169; H. Schulze, *Lehrbuch des deutschen Staatsrechts*, I, p. 368; Stahl, *Staatslehre*, 4. Aufl., p. 523; Taine, *loc. cit.: La révolution*, I, p. 274: "Ici rien de semblable aux déclarations précises de la Constitution américaine." In addition, note 1: *cf. la Déclaration d'indépendance du 4 juillet 1776*.

more fitting object of comparison, the first amendments to the constitution of the United States,[6] and even imagine that the latter exerted some influence upon the French Declaration, in spite of the fact that they did not come into existence until after August 26, 1789. This error has arisen from the French Declaration of 1789 having been embodied word for word in the Constitution of September 3, 1791, and so to one not familiar with French constitutional history, and before whom only the texts of the constitutions themselves are lying, it seems to bear a later date.

By practically all those, however, who look further back than the French Declaration it is asserted that the Declaration of Independence of the United States on July 4, 1776, contains the first exposition of a series of rights of man.[7]

---

[6] Stahl, *loc. cit.*, p. 524; Taine, *loc. cit.* The fact that Jefferson's proposal to enact a declaration of rights was rejected is expressly emphasized in a note.

[7] Stahl, *loc. cit.*, p. 523, does mention, in addition, the declarations of the separate states, but he does not specify when they originated, nor in what relation they stand to the French

Yet the American Declaration of Independence contains only a single paragraph that resembles a declaration of rights. It reads as follows:

"We hold these truths to be self-evident, that all men are created equal, that they are endowed by their Creator with certain unalienable Rights, that among these are Life, Liberty and the pursuit of Happiness; That to secure these rights, Governments are instituted among Men, deriving their just powers from the consent of the governed; That whenever any Form of Government becomes destructive of these ends, it is the Right of the People to alter or to abolish it, and to institute new Government, laying its foundation on such principles and organizing its powers in such form, as to them shall seem most likely to effect their Safety and Happiness."

Declaration, and his comments show that he is not at all familiar with them. Janet, *loc. cit.*, I, p. v *et seq.*, enters at length into the subject of the state declarations in order to show the originality of the French, and he even makes the mistaken attempt to prove French influence upon the American (p. xxxv). The more detailed history of the American declarations he is quite ignorant of.

This sentence is so general in its content that it is difficult to read into it, or deduct from it, a whole system of rights. It is therefore, at the very start, improbable that it served as the model for the French Declaration.

This conjecture becomes a certainty through Lafayette's own statement. In a place in his *Memoirs*, that has as yet been completely overlooked, Lafayette mentions the model that he had in mind when making his motion in the Constituent Assembly.[8] He very pertinently points out that the Congress of the newly formed Confederation of North American free states was then in no position to set up, for the separate colonies, which had already become sovereign states, rules of right which would have binding force. He brings out the fact that in the Declaration of Independence there are asserted only the principles of the sovereignty of the people and the right to change the form of government. Other rights are included solely by implication from the enumeration of the violations of right, which justified the separation from the mother country.

[8] *Mémoires, correspondances et manuscripts du général Lafayette, publiés par sa famille*, II, p. 46.

The constitutions of the separate states, however, were preceded by declarations of rights, which were binding upon the people's representatives. *The first state to set forth a declaration of rights properly so called was Virginia.*[9]

The declarations of Virginia and of the other individual American states were the sources of Lafayette's proposition. They influenced not only Lafayette, but all who sought to bring about a declaration of rights. Even the above-mentioned *cahiers* were affected by them.

The new constitutions of the separate American states were well known at that time in France. As early as 1778 a French translation of them, dedicated to Franklin, had appeared in Switzerland.[10] Another

---

[9] "Mais les constitutions que se donnèrent successivement les treize états, furent précedées de déclarations des droits, dont les principes devaient servir de règles aux représentans du peuple, soit aux conventions, soit dans les autres exercises de leur pouvoirs. La Virginie fut la première à produire une déclaration des droits proprement dite."—*Ibid.*, p. 47.

[10] *Recueil des loix constitutives des colonies angloises, confédérées sous la dénomination d'États-*

was published in 1783 at Benjamin Franklin's own instigation.[11] Their influence upon the constitutional legislation of the French Revolution is by no means sufficiently recognized. In Europe until quite recently only the Federal constitution was known, not the constitutions of the individual states, which are assuming a very prominent place in modern constitutional history. This must be evident from the fact, which is even yet unrecognized by some distinguished historians and teachers of public law, that the individual American states had the first written constitutions. In England and France the importance of the American state constitutions has begun to be appreciated,[12] but in Germany they have remained as yet

Unis de l'Amérique-Septentrionale. Dédié à M. le Docteur Franklin. En suisse, chez les libraires associés.

[11] Cf. Ch. Borgeaud, Établissement et revision des constitutions en Amérique et en Europe, Paris, 1893, p. 27.

[12] Especially the exceptional work of James Bryce, The American Commonwealth, Vol I, Part II., The State Governments; Boutmy, Études de droit constitutionnel, 2me éd., Paris, 1895, pp. 83 et seq.; and Borgeaud, loc. cit., pp. 28 et seq.

almost unnoticed. For a long time, to be sure, the text of the older constitutions in their entirety were only with difficulty accessible in Europe. But through the edition, prepared by order of the United States Senate,[13] containing all the American constitutions since the very earliest period, one is now in a position to become acquainted with these exceptionally important documents.

The French Declaration of Rights is for the most part copied from the American declarations or "bills of rights".[14] All drafts of the French Declaration, from those of the *cahiers* to the twenty-one proposals before the National Assembly, vary more or less from the original, either in conciseness or in breadth, in cleverness or in awkwardness of

---

[13] *The Federal and State Constitutions, Colonial Charters, and other Organic Laws of the United States.* Compiled by Ben: Perley Poore. Two vols., Washington, 1877. Only the most important documents of the colonial period are included.

[14] This is not quite clear even to the best French authority on American history, Laboulaye, as is evident from his treatment of the subject, *Histoire des États-Unis*, II, p. 11.

expression. But so far as substantial additions are concerned they present only doctrinaire statements of a purely theoretical nature or elaborations, which belong to the realm of political metaphysics. To enter upon them here is unnecessary. Let us confine ourselves to the completed work, the Declaration as it was finally determined after long debate in the sessions from the twentieth to the twenty-sixth of August.[15]

[15] *Cf. Arch. Parl.*, VIII, pp. 461–489.

CHAPTER IV.

VIRGINIA'S BILL OF RIGHTS AND THOSE OF THE OTHER NORTH AMERICAN STATES.

THE Congress of the colonies, which were already resolved upon separation from the mother country, while sitting in Philadelphia issued on May 15, 1776, an appeal to its constituents to give themselves constitutions. Of the thirteen states that originally made up the Union, eleven had responded to this appeal before the outbreak of the French Revolution. Two retained the colonial charters that had been granted them by the English crown, and invested these documents with the character of constitutions, namely, Connecticut the charter of 1662, and Rhode Island that of 1663, so that these charters are the oldest written constitutions in the modern sense.[1]

[1] Connecticut in 1818, and Rhode Island first in 1842, put new constitutions in the place of the old Colonial Charters.

Of the other states Virginia was the first to enact a constitution in the convention which met at Williamsburg from May 6 to June 29, 1776. It was prefaced with a formal "bill of rights",[2] which had been adopted by the convention on the twelfth of June. The author of this document was George Mason, although Madison exercised a decided influence upon the form that was finally adopted.[3] This declaration of Virginia's served as a pattern for all the others, even for that of the Congress of the United States, which was issued three weeks later, and, as is well known, was drawn up by Jefferson, a citizen of Virginia. In the other declarations there were many stipulations formulated somewhat differently, and also many new particulars were added.[4]

[2] Poore, II, pp. 1908, 1909.
[3] On the origin of Virginia's bill of rights, *cf.* Bancroft, *History of the United States*, London, 1861, VII, chap. 64.
[4] Virginia's declaration has 16, that of Massachusetts 30, and Maryland's 42 articles. Virginia's declaration does not include the right of emigration, which was first enacted in Article XV of Pennsylvania's; the rights of assembling and petition are also lacking, which were first found in the Pennsylvania bill of rights (Article XVI).

Express declarations of rights had been formulated after Virginia's before 1789 in the constitutions of

> Pennsylvania of September 28, 1776,
> Maryland of November 11, 1776,
> North Carolina of December 18, 1776,
> Vermont of July 8, 1777,[5]
> Massachusetts of March 2, 1780,
> New Hampshire of October 31, 1783,
>   (in force June 2, 1784.)

In the oldest constitutions of New Jersey, South Carolina, New York and Georgia special bills of rights are wanting, although they contain many provisions which belong in that category.[6] The French translation of the American Constitutions of 1778 includes a *déclaration expositive des droits* by

---

[5] Vermont's statehood was contested until 1790, and it was first recognized February 18, 1791, as an independent member of the United States.

[6] Religious liberty is recognized by New York in an especially emphatic manner, Constitution of April 20, 1777, Art. XXXVIII. Poore, II, p. 1338.

Delaware that is lacking in Poore's collection.[7]

In the following section the separate articles of the French Declaration are placed in comparison with the corresponding articles from the American declarations. Among the latter, however, I have sought out only those that most nearly approach the form of expression in the French text. But it must be once more strongly emphasized that the fundamental ideas of the American declarations generally duplicate each other, so that the same stipulation reappears in different form in the greater number of the bills of rights.

We shall leave out the introduction with which the Constituent Assembly prefaced its declaration, and begin at once with the enumeration of the rights themselves. But even the introduction, in which the National Assembly "*en présence et sous les auspices de l'Être suprême*" solemnly proclaims the recognition and declaration of the rights of

[7] Pp. 151 *et seq.*
(The translator has reprinted this declaration in an article in the *American Historical Review*, of July, 1898, entitled "The Delaware Bill of Rights of 1776".)

man and of citizens, and also sets forth the significance of the same, is inspired by the declaration of Congress and by those of many of the individual states with which the Americans sought to justify their separation from the mother country.

CHAPTER V.

COMPARISON OF THE FRENCH AND AMERICAN DECLARATIONS.

DÉCLARATION DES DROITS DE L'HOMME ET DU CITOYEN.	AMERICAN BILLS OF RIGHTS.
ART. 1. *Les hommes naissent et demeurent libres et égaux en droits. Les distinctions sociales ne peuvent être fondées que sur l'utilité commune.* 2. *Le but de toute association politique est la conservation des droits naturels et imprescriptibles de l'homme. Ces droits sont la liberté, la propriété, la sûreté et*	VIRGINIA, I. That all men are by nature equally free and independent, and have certain inherent rights, of which, when they enter into a state of society, they cannot, by any compact, deprive or divest their posterity; namely, the enjoyment of life and liberty, with the means of acquiring and possessing property, and

la résistance à l'oppression.

pursuing and obtaining happiness and safety.

VIRGINIA, IV. That no man, or set of men, are entitled to exclusive or separate emoluments or privileges from the community, but in consideration of public services.

MASSACHUSETTS, Preamble to the Constitution. The end of the institution, maintenance, and administration of government is to secure the existence of the body-politic, to protect it, and to furnish the individuals who compose it with the power of enjoying, in safety and tranquillity, their natural rights and the blessings of life.

3. *Le principe de toute souveraineté réside essentiellement dans la nation. Nul corps, nul individu ne peut exercer d'autorité qui n'en émane expréssement.*

4. *La liberté consiste à pouvoir faire tout ce qui ne nuit pas à autrui; aussi l'exercise des droits naturels de chaque homme n'a de bornes que celles qui assurent aux autres membres de la société la jouis-*

MARYLAND, IV. The doctrine of non-resistance, against arbitrary power and oppression, is absurd, slavish and destructive of the good and happiness of mankind.

VIRGINIA, II. That all power is vested in, and consequently derived from, the people; that magistrates are their trustees and servants, and at all times amenable to them.

MASSACHUSETTS, Preamble. The body-politic is formed by a voluntary association of individuals; it is a social compact by which the whole people covenants with each citizen and each citizen with the

sance de ces mêmes droits. Ces bornes ne peuvent être déterminées que par la loi.

5. *La loi n'a le droit de défendre que les actions nuisibles à la société. Tout ce qui n'est pas défendu par la loi ne peut être empêché et nul ne peut être contraint à faire ce qu'elle n'ordonne pas.*

whole people that all shall be governed by certain laws for the common good.

MASSACHUSETTS, X. Each individual of the society has a right to be protected by it in the enjoyment of his life, liberty, and property, according to standing laws.

MASSACHUSETTS, XI. Every subject of the commonwealth ought to find a certain remedy, by having recourse to the laws, for all injuries or wrongs which he may receive in his person, property, or character.

NORTH CAROLINA XIII. That every freeman, restrained of his liberty, is entitled to a remedy, to inquire into the lawfulness thereof, and to remove the same, if unlawful; and that such remedy ought not to be denied or delayed.

VIRGINIA, VII. That all power of suspending laws, or the execution of laws, by any authority, without consent of the representatives of the people, is injurious to their rights, and ought not to be exercised.[1]

6. *La loi est l'expression de la volonté générale. Tous les citoyens ont le droit de concourir personnellement ou par leurs représentants à sa formation. Elle doit*

MARYLAND, V. That the right in the people to participate in the Legislature, is the best security of liberty, and the foundation of all free government.

[1] *Cf.* English Bill of Rights, 1.

être la même pour tous, soit qu'elle protège, soit qu'elle punisse. Tous les citoyens étant égaux à ses yeux, sont également admissibles à toutes dignités, *places et emplois publics*, selon leur capacité, et sans autre distinction que celle de leurs vertus et leurs talents.

MASSACHUSETTS, IX. All elections ought to be free;[2] and all the inhabitants of this commonwealth, having such qualifications as they shall establish by their frame of government, have an equal right to elect officers, and to be elected, for public employments.

NEW HAMPSHIRE, XII. Nor are the inhabitants of this State controllable by any other laws than those to which they or their representative body have given their consent.

✗ Nul homme ne peut être accusé, arrêté, ni détenu que

MASSACHUSETTS, XII. No subject shall be held to answer for

---

[2] English Bill of Rights, 8

AND AMERICAN DECLARATIONS. 33

dans les cas déterminés par la loi et selon les formes qu'elle a prescrites. Ceux qui sollicitent, expédient, exécutent ou font exécuter des ordres arbitraires, doivent être punis ; mais tout citoyen appelé ou saisi en vertu de la loi doit obéir à l'instant ; il se rend coupable par sa résistance.

any crimes or no offence until the same is fully and plainly, substantially and formally, described to him; or be compelled to accuse, or furnish evidence against himself; and every subject shall have a right to produce all proofs that may be favorable to him; to meet the witnesses against him face to face, and to be fully heard in his defence by himself, or his counsel at his election. And no subject shall be arrested, imprisoned, despoiled, or deprived of his property, immunities, or privileges, put out of the protection of the law, exiled or deprived of his life, liberty, or estate, but by the judgment of his peers, or the law of the land.[3]

VIRGINIA, X. That general warrants, whereby an officer or messenger may be commanded to search suspected places without evidence of a fact committed, or to seize any person or persons not named, or whose offence is not particularly described and supported by evidence, are grievous and oppressive, and ought not to be granted.

X. *La loi ne doit établir que des peines strictement nécessaires et nul ne peut être puni qu'en vertu*

NEW HAMPSHIRE, XVIII. All penalties ought to be proportioned to the nature of the offence.[4]

---

[3] Magna Charta, 39.

[4] Magna Charta, 20.

d'une loi établie et promulguée antérieurement au délit et légalement appliquée.

MARYLAND, XIV. That sanguinary laws ought to be avoided, as far as is consistent with the safety of the State; and no law, to inflict cruel and unusual pains and penalties, ought to be made in any case, or at any time hereafter.[5]

MARYLAND, XV. That retrospective laws, punishing facts committed before the existence of such laws, and by them only declared criminal, are oppressive, unjust, and incompatible with liberty; wherefore no *ex post facto* law ought to be made.

Tout homme

Cf. above, MAS-

---

[5] English Bill of Rights, 10.

étant présumé innocent jusqu'à ce qu'il ait été déclaré coupable, s'il est jugé indispensable de l'arrêter, toute rigueur qui ne serait pas nécessaire pour s'assurer de sa personne doit être sévèrement réprimée par la loi.

10. Nul doit être inquiété pour ses opinions, même religieuses, pourvu que leur manifestation ne trouble pas l'ordre public établi par la loi.

SACHUSETTS, XII; further

MASSACHUSETTS, XIV. Every subject has a right to be secure from all unreasonable searches and seizures of his person, his houses, his papers, and all his possessions.

MASSACHUSETTS, XXVI. No magistrate or court of law shall demand excessive bail or sureties, impose excessive fines [6] . . .

NEW HAMPSHIRE, V. Every individual has a natural and unalienable right to worship GOD according to the dictates of his own conscience, and reason; and no

---

[6] English Bill of Rights, 10.

subject shall be hurt, molested or restrained in his person, liberty or estate for worshipping GOD, in the manner and season most agreeable to the dictates of his own conscience, or for his religious profession, sentiments or persuasion; provided he doth not disturb the public peace, or disturb others, in their religious worship.

11. La libre communication des pensées et des opinions est un des droits les plus précieux de l'homme; tout citoyen peut donc parler, écrire, imprimer librement sauf à répondre de l'abus de cette liberté dans les

VIRGINIA, XII. That the freedom of the press is one of the great bulwarks of liberty, and can never be restrained but by despotic governments.

PENNSYLVANIA, XII. That the people have a right to free-

cas determinés par la loi.

12. *La garantie des droits de l'homme et du citoyen nécessité une force publique. Cette force est donc instituée pour l'avantage de tous, et non pour l'utilité particulière de ceux auxquels elle est confiée.*

13. *Pour l'entretien de la force publique et pour les dépenses d'administration, une contribution commune est indispensable; elle doit être également répartie entre tous les*

dom of speech, and of writing, and publishing their sentiments.

PENNSYLVANIA, V. That government is, or ought to be, instituted for the common benefit, protection and security of the people, nation or community; and not for the particular emolument or advantage of any single man, family, or sett of men, who are a part only of that community.

MASSACHUSETTS, X. Each individual of the society has a right to be protected by it in the enjoyment of his life, liberty, and property, according to standing laws. He is obliged,

citoyens en raison de leurs facultés.

14. *Tous les citoyens ont le droit de constater, par eux mêmes ou par leur représentants, la nécessité de la contribution publique, de la consentir librement, d' en suivre l' emploi, et d' en déterminer la qualité, l' assiette, le recouvrement et la durée.*

15. *La société a le droit de demander compte à tout agent public de son administration.*

consequently, to contribute his share to the expense of this protection; to give his personal service, or an equivalent, when necessary.

MASSACHUSETTS, XXIII. No subsidy, charge, tax, impost, or duties, ought to be established, fixed, laid or levied, under any pretext whatsoever, without the consent of the people, or their representatives in the legislature.

See above, VIRGINIA, II; further

MASSACHUSETTS V. All power residing originally in the people, and being derived from them, the several magis-

16. *Toute société, dans laquelle la garantie des droits n'est pas assurée, ni la séparation des pouvoirs déterminée, n'a point de constitution.*

trates and officers of government vested with authority, whether legislative, executive, or judicial, are the substitutes and agents, and are at all times accountable to them.

NEW HAMPSHIRE, III. When men enter into a state of society, they surrender up some of their natural rights to that society, in order to insure the protection of others; and without such an equivalent, the surrender is void.

MASSACHUSETTS, XXX. In the government of this commonwealth, the legislative department shall never exercise the executive and judicial powers, or either of them; the executive shall never exercise the legislative and judicial powers, or either of them; the judicial shall never exercise the legislative and executive powers, or either of them; to the end it may be a government of laws, and not of men.

17. *La propriété étant un droit inviolable et sacré, nul ne peut en être privé, si ce n'est lors que la nécessité publique, légalement constatée, l'exige évidemment, et sous la condition d'une juste et préalable indemnité.*

MASSACHUSETTS, X. . . . But no part of the property of any individual can, with justice, be taken from him, or applied to public uses, without his own consent, or that of the representative body of the people. . . . And whenever the public exigencies require that the property of any individual should be appropriated to public uses, he shall receive a reasonable compensation therefor.

VERMONT, II. That private property ought to be subservient to public uses, when necessity requires it; nevertheless, whenever any particular man's property is taken for the use of the public, the owner ought to receive an equivalent in money.

CHAPTER VI.

THE CONTRAST BETWEEN THE AMERICAN AND ENGLISH DECLARATIONS OF RIGHTS.

THE comparison of the American and French declarations shows at once that the setting forth of principles abstract, and therefore ambiguous, is common to both, as is also the pathos with which they are recited. The French have not only adopted the American ideas, but even the form they received on the other side of the ocean. But in contrast to the diffuseness of the Americans the French are distinguished by a brevity characteristic of their language. Articles 4–6 of the Declaration have the most specific French additions in the superfluous and meaningless definitions of liberty[1]

---

[1] It harks back finally to the old definition of Florentinus L. 4 D. 1, 5: "Libertas est naturalis facultas eius, quod cuique facere libet, nisi si quid vi aut jure prohibetur."

and law. Further, in Articles 4, 6 and 13 of the French text special stress is laid upon equality before the law, while to the Americans, because of their social conditions and democratic institutions, this seemed self-evident and so by them is only brought out incidentally. In the French articles the influence of the *Contrat Social* is seen; but yet it brought out nothing essentially new, or unknown to the American stipulations.

The result that has been won is not without significance for the student of history in passing judgment upon the effects of the French Declaration. The American states have developed with their bills of rights into orderly commonwealths in which there has never been any complaint that these propositions brought consequences disintegrating to the state. The disorders which arose in France after the Declaration of the Rights of Man cannot therefore have been brought about by its formulas alone. Much rather do they show what dangers may lie in the too hasty adoption of foreign institutions. That is, the Americans in 1776 went on building upon foundations that were with them long-standing. The French, on the other hand, tore up all the foundations of their state's structure. What was in the one case a factor in the process of consolidation served in the other as a cause of further disturbance. This was even recognized at the time by sharp-sighted men, such as Lally-Tollendal [2] and, above all, Mirabeau. [3]

But from the consideration of the American bills of rights there arises a new problem for the historian of law: How did Americans come to make legislative declarations of this sort?

To the superficial observer the answer seems simple. The very name points to English sources. The Bill of Rights of 1689, the Habeas Corpus Act of 1679, the Petition of Right of 1628, and finally the *Magna Charta libertatum* appear to be unquestionably the predecessors of the Virginia bill of rights.

Assuredly the remembrance of these celebrated English enactments, which the Americans regarded as an inherent part of the law of their land, had a substantial share in the declarations of rights after 1776. Many stipulations from Magna Charta and the English

[2] *Arch. parl.* VIII, p. 222.
[3] *Ibid.*, pp. 438 and 453.

Bill of Rights were directly embodied by the Americans in their lists.

And yet a deep cleft separates the American declarations from the English enactments that have been mentioned. The historian of the American Revolution says of the Virginia declaration that it protested against all tyranny in the name of the eternal laws of man's being: "The English petition of right in 1688 was historic and retrospective; the Virginia declaration came directly out of the heart of nature and announced governing principles for all peoples in all future times."[4]

The English laws that establish the rights of subjects are collectively and individually confirmations, arising out of special conditions, or interpretations of existing law. Even Magna Charta contains no new right, as Sir Edward Coke, the great authority on English law, perceived as early as the beginning of the seventeenth century.[5] The English statutes are far removed from any purpose to recognize general rights of man, and they have neither the power nor the in-

---

[4] Bancroft, VII, p. 243.

[5] *Cf.* Blackstone, *Commentaries on the Laws of England*, I, 1, p. 127. (Edited by Kerr, London, 1887, I, p. 115.)

tention to restrict the legislative agents or to establish principles for future legislation. According to English law Parliament is omnipotent and all statutes enacted or confirmed by it are of equal value.

The American declarations, on the other hand, contain precepts which stand higher than the ordinary lawmaker. In the Union, as well as in the individual states, there are separate organs for ordinary and for constitutional legislation, and the judge watches over the observance of the constitutional limitations by the ordinary legislative power. If in his judgment a law infringes on the fundamental rights, he must forbid its enforcement. The declarations of rights even at the present day are interpreted by the Americans as practical protections of the minority.[6] This distinguishes them from the "guaranteed rights" of the European states.

[6] Upon this point, *cf.* Cooley, *Constitutional Limitations*, 6th edition, Boston, 1890, Chap. VII. Even if the stipulation contained in the bills of rights that one can be deprived of his property only "by the law of the land" should not be embodied in the constitution by a state, a law transgressing it would be void by virtue of the fundamental limitations upon the competence of the legislatures. *Loc. cit.*, p. 208.

The American declarations are not laws of a higher kind in name only, they are the creations of a higher lawmaker. In Europe, it is true, the constitutions place formal difficulties in the way of changing their specifications, but almost everywhere it is the lawmaker himself who decides upon the change. Even in the Swiss Confederacy judicial control over the observance of these forms is nowhere to be found, although there, as in the United States, the constitutional laws proceed from other organs than those of the ordinary statutes.

The American bills of rights do not attempt merely to set forth certain principles for the state's organization, but they seek above all to draw the boundary line between state and individual. According to them the individual is not the possessor of rights through the state, but by his own nature he has inalienable and indefeasible rights. The English laws know nothing of this. They do not wish to recognize an eternal, natural right, but one inherited from their fathers, "the old, undoubted rights of the English people."

The English conception of the rights of the subject is very clear upon this point.

When one looks through the Bill of Rights carefully, one finds but slight mention there of individual rights. That laws should not be suspended, that there should be no dispensation from them, that special courts should not be erected, that cruel punishments should not be inflicted, that jurors ought to be duly impanelled and returned, that taxes should not be levied without a law, nor a standing army kept without consent of Parliament, that parliamentary elections should be free, and Parliament be held frequently, —all these are not rights of the individual, but duties of the government. Of the thirteen articles of the Bill of Rights only two contain stipulations that are expressed in the form of rights of the subject,[7] while one refers to freedom of speech in Parliament. When nevertheless all the stipulations of the Bill of Rights are therein designated as rights and liberties of the English people,[8] it is

---

[7] The right to address petitions to the king (5), and the right of Protestant subjects to carry arms for their own defense suitable to their condition (7).

[8] "And they do claim, demand, and insist upon all and singular the premises, as their undoubted rights and liberties."

through the belief that restriction of the crown is at the same time right of the people.

This view grew directly out of the mediæval conception of the Teutonic state. While the ancient state appears at the beginning of its history as πόλις or *civitas*, as an undivided community of citizens, the monarchical Teutonic state is from the beginning dualistic in form,—prince and people form no integral unity, but stand opposed to each other as independent factors. And so the state in the conception of the time is substantially a relation of contract between the two. The Roman and Canonical theory of law under the influence of ancient traditions even as early as the eleventh century attempts to unite the two elements in that, upon the basis of a contract, it either makes the people part with their rights to the prince, and accordingly makes the government the state, or it considers the prince simply as the authorized agent of the people and so makes the latter and the state identical. The prevailing opinion in public law, however, especially since the rise of the state of estates, sees in the state a double condition of contract between prince and people. The laws form the content of this compact. They established, therefore, for the prince a right of demanding lawful obedience, and for the people of demanding adherence to the limitations placed by the laws. The people accordingly have a right to the fulfilment of the law by the prince. Thus all laws create personal rights of the people, and the term people is thought of in a confused way as referring to the individuals as well as to the whole—*singuli et universi*.[9] From this point of view it is a right of the people that Parliament should be frequently summoned, that the judge should inflict no cruel punishments, and however else the declarations of the English charters may read.

This conception of law as two-sided, establishing rights for both elements of the state, runs through all the earlier English history. The right which is conferred by law passes from generation to generation, it becomes hereditary and therefore acquirable by birth

[9] The old English charters put forward as possessors of the "*jura et libertates*" now the "*homines in regno nostro*", now the *regnum* itself. The Petition of Right speaks of the "rights and liberties" of the subjects, but they are also characterized as "the laws and free customs of this realm".

as one of the people. Under Henry VI. it is declared of the law: "La ley est le plus haute inheritance que le roy ad; car par la ley il même et toutes ses sujets sont rulés, et si la ley ne fuit, nul roy et nul inheritance sera."[10] And in the Petition of Right Parliament makes the appeal that the subjects have inherited their freedom through the laws.[11] The laws, as the Act of Settlement expresses it, are the "birthright of the people".[12]

And so we find only ancient "rights and liberties" mentioned in the English laws of

[10] Year Books XIX, Gneist, *Englische Verfassungsgeschichte*, p. 450.

[11] "By which the statutes before-mentioned, and other the good laws and statutes of this realm, your subjects have inherited this freedom." Gardiner, *The Constitutional Documents of the Puritan Revolution*, 1889, pp. 1, 2.

[12] "And whereas the laws of England are the birthright of the people thereof." Act of Settlement IV, Stubbs, *Select Charters*, 7th ed., 1890, p. 531. Birthright = right by birth, the rights, privileges or possessions to which one is entitled by birth; inheritance, patrimony (specifically used of the special rights of the first-born). Murray, *A New English Dictionary on Historical Principles*, s. h. v.

the seventeenth century. Parliament is always demanding simply the confirmation of the "laws and statutes of this realm", that is, the strengthening of the existing relations between king and people. Of the creation of new rights there is not a word in all these documents. Consequently there is no reference whatever to the important fundamental rights of religious liberty, of assembling, of liberty of the press, or of free movement. And down to the present day the theory of English law does not recognize rights of this kind, but considers these lines of individual liberty as protected by the general principle of law, that any restraint of the person can only come about through legal authorization.[13] According to the present English idea the rights of liberty rest simply upon the supremacy of the law,—they are law, not personal rights.[14] The theory,

---

[13] *Cf.* the instructive work of Dicey, *Introduction to the Study of the Law of the Constitution*, 3d ed., 1889, pp. 171 *et seq.*

[14] "Sie sind objectives, nicht subjectives Recht." Dicey, pp. 184 *et seq.*, 193 *et seq.*, 223 *et seq.*, etc. Dicey treats the whole doctrine of the rights of liberty in the section "The Rule of Law." Individual liberty according to him is in

founded in Germany by Gerber, and defended by Laband and others, according to which the rights of liberty are nothing but duties of the government, sprang up in England, without any connection with the German teaching, from the existing conditions after the conception of the public rights of the individual as natural rights, which was based on Locke and Blackstone, had lost its power.

But with Locke even this conception stands in close connection with the old English ideas. When Locke considers property—in which are included life and liberty—as an original right of the individual existing previous to the state, and when he conceives of the state as a society founded to protect this right, which is thus transformed from a natural to a civil right, he by no means ascribes definite fundamental rights to the man living in the state, but rather places such positive restrictions upon the legislative power as follow from the purposes of the state.[15] When closely examined,

---

England simply the correlative of only permitting the restriction of the individual through laws.

[15] This is treated in the chapter "Of the Ex-

however, these restrictions are nothing else than the most important stipulations of the Bill of Rights, which was enacted the year before the *Two Treatises on Government* appeared.[16]

Blackstone was the first (1765) to found his doctrine of the absolute rights of persons upon the idea of the personal rights of the individual. Security, liberty, and property are the absolute rights of every Englishman, which from their character are nothing else than the natural liberty that remains to the individual after deducting the legal restraints demanded by the common interest.[17] Laws appear likewise as protectors of these rights, —the whole constitution of Parliament, the limitation of the royal prerogative, and along with these the protection of the law courts, the right of petition, and the right to carry arms are treated, exactly in the manner of

tent of the Legislative Power," *On Civil Government*, XI.

[16] *Cf. On Civil Government*, XI, § 142.

[17] Political liberty is no other than national liberty so far restrained by human laws (and no farther) as is necessary and expedient for the general advantage of the public. *Loc. cit.*, p. 125 (113).

the Bill of Rights, as rights of Englishmen, and indeed as subordinate rights to assist in guarding the three principal rights.[18] But in spite of his fundamental conception of a natural right, the individual with rights was for Blackstone not man simply, but the English subject.[19]

The American declarations of rights, on the other hand, begin with the statement that all men are born free and equal, and these declarations speak of rights that belong to "every individual", "all mankind" or "every member of society". They enumerate a much larger number of rights than the English declarations, and look upon these rights as innate and inalienable. Whence comes this conception in American law?

It is not from the English law. There is then nothing else from which to derive it than the conceptions of natural rights of that time. But there have been theories of natural rights ever since the time of the Greeks, and they never led to the formulation of fundamental rights. The theory of natural rights for a long time had no hesitation in setting forth the contradiction between nat-

---

[18] *Loc. cit.*, pp. 141 *et seq.* (127 *et seq.*).
[19] *Cf. loc. cit.*, pp. 127 (114), 144 (130).

ural law and positive law without demanding the realization of the former through the latter. A passage from Ulpian is drawn upon in the *Digests*, which declares all men to be equal according to the law of nature, but slavery to be an institution of the civil law.[20] The Romans, however, in spite of all mitigation of slave laws, never thought of such a thing as the abolition of slavery. The natural freedom of man was set forth by many writers during the eighteenth century as compatible with lawful servitude. Even Locke, for whom liberty forms the very essence of man, in his constitution for North Carolina sanctioned slavery and servitude.

Literature alone never produces anything, unless it finds in the historical and social conditions ground ready for its working. When one shows the literary origin of an idea, one has by no means therewith discovered the record of its practical significance. The history of political science to-day is entirely too much a history of the literature and too little a history of the institutions themselves. The number of new political

---

[20] L. 32 D. de R. J. Exactly so the kindred doctrines of the Stoics earlier in Greece had not the least legal success.

ideas is very small; the most, at least in embryo, were known to the ancient theories of the state. But the institutions are found in constant change and must be seized in their own peculiar historical forms.

CHAPTER VII.

RELIGIOUS LIBERTY IN THE ANGLO-AMERICAN COLONIES THE SOURCE OF THE IDEA OF ESTABLISHING BY LAW A UNIVERSAL RIGHT OF MAN.

THE democratic idea, upon which the constitution of the Reformed Church is based, was carried to its logical conclusion in England toward the end of the sixteenth century, and first of all by Robert Browne and his followers. They declared the Church, which was identical with the parish, to be a community of believers who had placed themselves under obedience to Christ by a compact with God, and they steadfastly recognized as authoritative only the will of the community at the time being, that is, the will of the majority.[1] Persecuted in England Brownism transformed itself on Dutch soil,

[1] Weingarten, *Die Revolutionskirchen Englands*, p. 21.

especially through the agency of John Robinson, into Congregationalism, in which the earliest form of the Independent movement made its appearance. The principles of Congregationalism are first complete separation of Church and State and then the autonomy of each separate parish,—as a petition addressed to James I. in 1616 expresses it: the right is exercised "of spiritual administration and government in itself and over itself by the common and free consent of the people, independently and immediately under Christ."[2]

This sovereign individualism in the religious sphere led to practical consequences of extraordinary importance. From its principles there finally resulted the demand for, and the recognition of, full and unrestricted liberty of conscience, and then the asserting of this liberty to be a right not granted by any earthly power and therefore by no earthly power to be restrained.

But the Independent movement could not confine itself to ecclesiastical matters, it was forced by logical necessity to carry its fundamental doctrines into the political sphere.

---

[2] *Ibid.*, p. 25.

As the Church, so it considered the state and every political association as the result of a compact between its original sovereign members.[3] This compact was made indeed in pursuance of divine commandment, but it remained always the ultimate legal basis of the community. It was concluded by virtue of the individual's original right and had not only to insure security and advance the general welfare, but above all to recognize and protect the innate and inalienable rights of conscience. And it is the entire people that specifically man for man concluded this compact, for by it alone could every one be bound to respect the self-created authority and the self-created law.

The first indications of these religious-political ideas can be traced far back, for they

[3] The connection of the Puritan-Independent doctrine of the state-compact with the Puritan idea of church covenants is brought out by Borgeaud, p. 9. Weingarten (p. 288) remarks forcibly of the Independents, "The right of every separate religious community freely and alone to decide and conduct their affairs was the foundation of the doctrine of the sovereignty of the people, which they introduced into the political consciousness of the modern world."

were not created by the Reformation. But the practice which developed on the basis of these ideas was something unique. For the first time in history social compacts, by which states are founded, were not merely demanded, they were actually concluded. What had until then slumbered in the dust-covered manuscripts of the scholar became a powerful, life-determining movement. The men of that time believed that the state rested upon a contract, and they put their belief into practice. More recent theory of public law with only an imperfect knowledge of these events frequently employed them as examples of the possibility of founding a state by contract, without suspecting that these contracts were only the realization of an abstract theory.

On October 28, 1647, there was laid before the assembled Council of Cromwell's army a draft, worked out by the Levellers, of a new constitution for England,[4] which later, greatly enlarged and modified,[5] was

---

[4] First reproduced in Gardiner, *History of the Great Civil War*, III, London, 1891, pp. 607–609.

[5] The final text in Gardiner, *Constitutional*

delivered to Parliament with the request that it be laid before the entire English people for signature.[6] In this remarkable document the power of Parliament was set forth as limited in a manner similar to that later adopted by the Americans, and particulars were enumerated which in future should not lie within the legislative power of the people's representatives. The first thing named was matters of religion, which were to be committed exclusively to the command of conscience.[7] They were reckoned among the inherent rights, the "native rights", which the people were firmly resolved to maintain with their utmost strength against all attacks.[8]

Here for the first and last time in England was an inherent right of religious liberty asserted in a proposed law. This right is recognized to-day in England in legal practice, but not in any expressly formulated principle.[9]

Documents of the Puritan Revolution, Oxford, 1889, pp. 270–282.

[6] Gardiner, *History*, III, p. 568.

[7] "That matters of religion and the ways of God's worship are not at all entrusted by us to any human power." Gardiner, *History*, p. 608.

[8] *Cf.* the text in Gardiner, *History*, p. 609.

[9] *Cf.* Dicey, *loc. cit.*, pp. 229, 230, where

The religious conditions in England's North American colonies developed differently.

The compact is celebrated which the persecuted and exiled Pilgrim Fathers concluded on board the Mayflower, November 11, 1620, before the founding of New Plymouth. Forty-one men on that occasion signed an act in which, for the glory of God, the advancement of the Christian faith, and the honor of their king and country, they declare their purpose to found a colony. They thereupon mutually promised one another to unite themselves into a civil body politic, and, for the maintenance of good order and accomplishment of their proposed object, to make laws, to appoint officers, and to subject themselves to these.[10]

Therewith began the series of "Plantation

several laws are mentioned restricting the liberty of expressing religious opinion which are, however, obsolete, though they have never been formally repealed.

[10] The complete text in Poore, I, p. 931. That it was far from the intentions of the settlers to found an independent state is evident from the entire document, in which they characterize themselves as "subjects of our dread Sovereign Lord King James".

Covenants" which the English settlers, according to their ecclesiastical and political ideas, believed it necessary to make on founding a new colony. Here they are only to be considered in their connection with religious liberty.

In 1629 Salem, the second colony in Massachusetts, was founded by Puritans. Unmindful of the persecutions they themselves had suffered in their native land, they turned impatiently against such as did not agree with them in their religious ideas. Roger Williams, a young Independent, landed in Massachusetts in 1631 and was at once chosen by the community in Salem to be its minister. But he preached complete separation of Church and State, and demanded absolute religious liberty, not only for all Christians but also for Jews, Turks, and heathen. They should have in the state equal civil and political rights with believers. A man's conscience belongs exclusively to him, and not to the state.[11] Exiled and in

[11] On Williams, *cf.* Weingarten, pp. 36 *et seq.*, and 293, Bancroft, I, pp. 276 *et seq.*, Masson, *The Life of John Milton*, II, pp. 560 *et seq.* The advance of the Independent movement to unconditional freedom of faith is thoroughly discussed by Weingarten, pp. 110 *et seq.*

danger, Williams forsook Salem and with a faithful few founded, 1636, the city of Providence in the country of the Narragansett Indians, where all who were persecuted on account of their religion should find a refuge. In the original compact the seceders promised obedience to laws determined by a majority of themselves, but "only in civil things"—religion was to be in no way a subject of legislation.[12] Here for the first time was recognized the most unrestricted liberty of religious conviction, and that by a man who was himself glowing with religious feeling.

Nineteen settlers from Providence in 1638 founded Aquedneck, the second colony in the present state of Rhode Island, after having concluded a most remarkable compact: "We whose names are underwritten do here solemnly, in the presence of Jehovah, incorporate ourselves into a Bodie Politik, and as he shall help, will submit our persons, lives and estates unto our Lord Jesus Christ, the King of Kings and Lord of Lords, and to all those perfect and absolute laws of his given us in his holy word of truth, to be

[12] Samuel Greene Arnold, *History of the State of Rhode Island*, I, New York, 1859, p. 103.

guided and judged hereby.—Exod. xxiv, 3, 4; 2 Chron. xi, 3; 2 Kings xi, 17." [13]

But such as did not go so far as Roger Williams in the recognition of liberty of conscience were yet dominated by the idea of the necessity of a social compact in founding a new colony. In the Fundamental Orders of Connecticut, a colony founded by Puritans who also had emigrated from Massachusetts, the settlers in 1638 declared that they united themselves in a body politic in pursuance of the word of God in order to guard the liberty of the Gospel and the church discipline to which they were accustomed, and in order also in civil affairs to be ruled according to the laws.[14] In the opposition in which they stood to the religious conditions in England, the Puritans, although themselves little inclined to toleration, proceeded invariably upon the idea that their state had first of all to realize religious liberty, which was for them the free exercise of their own religious convictions.

The idea that state and government rested upon a compact — so significant for the

[13] Arnold, p. 124.
[14] *Fundamental Orders of Connecticut*, Poore, I, p. 249.

development of the American conceptions of individual liberty—was strengthened by the force of historical circumstances. A handful of men went forth to found new communities. They began their work of civilization scattered over wide stretches in the loneliness of the primeval forest.[15] And so they believed that it was possible to live outside of the state, in a condition of nature, and that when they stepped out of that condition of nature they did it of their own free will and were not constrained by any earthly power. With their small numbers, representation was at first unnecessary, and the decisions were reached in the town meetings of all belonging to the community,—the form of a direct democracy grew naturally out of the given conditions and strengthened the conviction, which does not correspond to the old English conception, that the sovereignty of the people is the basis of legislation and of government. To a generation that could point to such beginnings for their state, the political ideas

[15] The entire number of immigrants in New England amounted in 1640 to 22,000 at the highest. Of these New Plymouth had 3000, Connecticut less than 2000 souls. Masson, *loc. cit.*, pp. 548–550.

which later animated the men of 1776 seemed to bear their surety in themselves: they were "self-evident", as it reads in the Declaration of Independence.

The inherent fundamental right of religious liberty, for which Roger Williams had striven so earnestly, found also in the seventeenth century its official recognition in law, first in the laws of 1647 of Rhode Island, and then in the charter which Charles II. granted the colony of Rhode Island and Providence Plantations in 1663.[16] It was therein ordered in fulfilment of the colonists' request, in a manner ever memorable, that in future in the said colony no person should be molested, punished or called in question for any differences of opinion in matters of religion; but that all persons at all times should have full liberty of conscience, so long as they behaved themselves peaceably and did not misuse this liberty in licentiousness or profaneness, nor

---

[16] The wide separation of the colonies from the mother-country did not make this liberty appear dangerous though it was in such contradiction to the conditions in England. Charles II. sought further, in his aversion to the Puritans, to favor as much as possible the colonies that had separated from Massachusetts.

to the injury or disturbance of others.[17] Thus a colony was granted that which in the mother-country at the time was contested to the utmost. Similar principles are found for the first time in Europe in the Practice of Frederick the Great in Prussia. But the principles of religious liberty were recognized to a greater or less extent in other colonies also. Catholic Maryland in 1649 granted freedom in the exercise of religion

[17] "Our royall will and pleasure is, that noe person within the sayd colonye, at any tyme hereafter, shall bee any wise molested, punished, disquieted, or called in question, for any differences in opinione in matters of religion, and doe not actually disturb the civill peace of our sayd colony; but that all and everye person and persons may, from tyme to tyme, and at all tymes hereafter, freelye and fullye have and enjoye his and their owne judgments and consciences, in matters of religious concernments, throughout the tract of lande hereafter mentioned; they behaving themselves peaceablie and quietlie, and not useing this libertie to lycentiousnesse and profanenesse, nor to the civill injurye or outward disturbeance of others; any lawe, statute or clause, therein contayned, or to bee contayned, usage or custome of this realme, to the contrary hereof, in any wise, notwithstanding." Poore, II, pp. 1596, 1597.

to every one who acknowledged Jesus Christ.[18] Also that remarkable constitution which Locke prepared for North Carolina and that went into force there in 1669, and which agrees so little with the tenets of his *Two Treatises on Government*, is based upon the principle not, it is true, of full equality of rights, but of toleration of Dissenters, and also of Jews and heathen.[19] It was permitted every seven persons of any religion to form a church or communion of faith.[20] No compulsion in matters of religion was exercised, except that every inhabitant when seventeen years of age had to declare to which communion he belonged and to be registered in some church, otherwise he stood outside of the protection of the law.[21] All violence toward any religious assembly was strictly prohibited.[22] It was not the principle of

[18] Bancroft, I, p. 193, E. Lloyd Harris, *Church and State in the Maryland Colony.* Inaugural-Dissertation. Heidelberg, 1894, p. 26 *et seq.*

[19] Carolina had already had religious toleration in the Charter of 1665. Poore, II, p. 1397. Locke himself wished to grant full religious liberty. *Cf.* Laboulaye, I, p. 397.

[20] Art. 97. Poore, II, pp. 1406, 1407.

[21] Art. 101. *Ibid.*

[22] Arts. 102, 106. *Ibid.*

political liberty that lay on Locke's heart, but the opening of a way to full religious liberty. In spite of the fact that in his treatise *On Civil Government* there is not a word upon the right of conscience, which he had so energetically defended in his celebrated *Letters on Toleration*, the constitution of North Carolina shows that in his practical plans it held the first place. And so with Locke also liberty of conscience was brought forward as the first and most sacred right, overshadowing all others. This philosopher, who held freedom to be man's inalienable gift from nature, established servitude and slavery under the government he organized without hesitation, but religious toleration he carried through with great energy in this new feudal state.

Of the other colonies New Jersey had proclaimed extensive toleration in 1664, and New York in 1665.[23] In the latter, which had already declared under Dutch rule in favor of liberal principles in religious matters, it was ordered in 1683 that no one who believed on Jesus Christ should on any pretext whatever be molested because of differ-

[23] C. Ellis Stevens, *Sources of the Constitution of the United States*, New York, 1894, p. 217.

ence of opinion. In the same year William Penn conferred a constitution with democratic basis upon the colony granted to him by the Crown and which he had named after his father Pennsylvania, in which it was declared that no one who believed on God should in any way be forced to take part in any religious worship or be otherwise molested,[24] and in the constitution, which Penn later (1701) established and which remained in force until 1776, he emphasized above all that even when a people were endowed with the greatest civil liberties they could not be truly happy, unless liberty of conscience were recognized,[25] and at the close he solemnly promised for himself and his heirs that the recognition of this liberty, which he had declared, should remain forever inviolable and that the wording of the article should not be changed in any particular.[26] The constitutional principle was thus given

[24] Laws agreed upon in England, Art. XXXV. Poore, II, p. 1526.

[25] Charter of Privileges for Pennsylvania, Art. I. Poore, II, p. 1537. For holding office the confession of belief in Jesus Christ as the Saviour of the world was necessary, but no special creed.

[26] Art. VIII, section 3.

at once the force of a *lex in perpetuum valitura*.

In 1692 Massachusetts received a charter from William III. in which, following the example of the Toleration Act of 1689, full liberty was granted to all Christians except Catholics;[27] and Georgia was given a similar law in 1732 by George II.[28]

Thus the principles of religious liberty to a greater or less extent acquired constitutional recognition in America. In the closest connection with the great religious political movement out of which the American democracy was born, there arose the conviction that there exists a right not conferred upon the citizen but inherent in man, that acts of conscience and expressions of religious conviction stand inviolable over against the state as the exercise of a higher right. This right so long suppressed is no "inheritance", is nothing handed down from their fathers, as the rights and liberties of Magna Charta and of the other English enactments,

---

[27] Poore, I, p. 950. On this point *cf.* Lauer, *Church and State in New England* in *Johns Hopkins University Studies, 10th Series*, II–III, Baltimore, 1892, pp. 35 *et seq.*

[28] Poore, I, p. 375.

—not the State but the Gospel proclaimed it.

What in Europe at that time and even much later had received official expression only in scanty rudiments,[29] and aside from that was only asserted in the literature of the great intellectual movement which began in the seventeenth century and reached its height in the clearing-up epoch of the century following, was in Rhode Island and other colonies a recognized principle of the state by the middle of the seventeenth century. The right of the liberty of conscience was proclaimed, and with it came the concep-

[29] In England the Toleration Act, I. Will. and Mary, c. 18, first granted toleration to Dissenters. This was again restricted under Anne and restored under George I. Since George II. they have been admitted to all offices. As is well known, however, the restrictions upon the Catholics and Jews have been done away with only in our century. In Germany after the scanty concessions of the Peace of Osnabrück, a state of affairs similar to that earlier in America was first created by the Toleration Patent of Joseph II. of 1781, the Edict of Frederick William II. of July 9, 1788, that which codified the principles of Frederick the Great, and above all by the Prussian *Allgemeines Landrecht* (Teil II, Titel 11, §§ 1 *et seq.*).

tion of a universal right of man. In 1776 this right was designated by all the bills of rights, mostly in emphatic form and with precedence over all others, as a natural and inherent right.[30]

[30] To be sure the carrying out of this right, in the direction of full political equality to the members of all confessions, differed in the different states. New York was the first state after Rhode Island that brought about the separation of church and state. Virginia followed next in 1785. For some time after in many states Protestant or at least Christian belief was necessary to obtain office. And even to-day some states require belief in God, in immortality, and in a future state of rewards and punishments. Massachusetts declared in her bill of rights not only the right but the duty of worship, and as late as 1799 punished neglect of church attendance. In the course of the nineteenth century these and other restrictions have fallen away except for a very small part. For the Union the exercise of political rights is made entirely independent of religious belief by Art. VI of the Constitution, and also by the famous First Amendment the establishment of any religion or prohibiting the free exercise thereof is forbidden. On the present condition in the separate states, *cf.* the thorough discussion by Cooley, Chap. XIII, pp. 541–586; further Rüttiman, *Kirche und Staat in Nordamerika* (1871).

The character of this right is emphasized by the bill of rights of New Hampshire, which declares that among the natural rights some are inalienable because no one can offer an equivalent for them. Such are the rights of conscience.[31]

The idea of legally establishing inalienable, inherent and sacred rights of the individual is not of political but religious origin. What has been held to be a work of the Revolution was in reality a fruit of the Reformation and its struggles. Its first apostle was not Lafayette but Roger Williams, who, driven by powerful and deep religious enthusiasm, went into the wilderness in order to found a government of religious liberty, and his name is uttered by Americans even to-day with the deepest respect.

[31] "Among the natural rights, some are in their very nature unalienable, because no equivalent can be given or received for them. Of this kind are the RIGHTS OF CONSCIENCE." Art. IV. Poore, II, 1280.

CHAPTER VIII.

THE CREATION OF A SYSTEM OF RIGHTS OF MAN AND OF CITIZENS DURING THE AMERICAN REVOLUTION.

THE seventeenth century was a time of religious struggles. In the following century political and economic interests pressed into the foreground of historical movement. The democratic institutions of the colonies were repeatedly in opposition to those of the mother-country, and the ties that bound them to her lost more and more of their significance. The great antagonism of their economic interests began to make itself widely felt. The economic prosperity of the colonies demanded the least possible restriction upon free movement. Finally they felt that they were ruled not by their old home but by a foreign country.

Then the old Puritan and Independent conceptions became effective in a new direction. The theory of the social compact which played so important a rôle in the founding of the colonies, and had helped to establish religious liberty, now supported in the most significant way the reconstruction of existing institutions. Not that it changed these institutions, it simply gave them a new basis.

The colonists had brought over the ocean with them their liberties and rights as English-born subjects. In a series of charters from the English kings it was specifically stated that the colonists and their descendants should enjoy all the rights which belonged to Englishmen in their native land.[1] Even before the English Bill of Rights the most of the colonies had enacted laws in which the ancient English liberties were gathered together.[2] There occurred, however, in the second half of the eighteenth century a great transformation in these old

---

[1] Kent, *Commentaries on American Law*, 10th ed., I, p. 611.

[2] *Cf.* Kent, I, pp. 612 *et seq.;* Stevens, *loc. cit.*, pp. 208 *et seq.* They are universally designated to-day in America as "bills of rights". Their example undoubtedly influenced the declarations of 1776 and those after.

rights. The inherited rights and liberties, as well as the privileges of organization, which had been granted the colonists by the English kings or had been sanctioned by the colonial lords, do not indeed change in word, but they become rights which spring not from man but from God and Nature.

To these ancient rights new ones were added. With the conviction that there existed a right of conscience independent of the State was found the starting-point for the determination of the inalienable rights of the individual. The theory of a Law of Nature recognized generally but one natural right of the individual—liberty or property. In the conceptions of the Americans, however, in the eighteenth century there appears a whole series of such rights.

The teaching of Locke, the theories of Pufendorf[3] and the ideas of Montesquieu, all

---

[3] Borgeaud, p. 27, cites a treatise by John Wyse as having had great influence in the democratizing of ideas in Massachusetts. This man, whose name was John Wise, has done nothing else than take Pufendorf's theories as the basis of his work, as he himself specifically declares. *Cf.* J. Wise, *A Vindication on the Government of New England Churches*, Boston. 1772, p. 22.

powerfully influenced the political views of the Americans of that time. But the setting forth of a complete series of universal rights of man and of citizens can in no way be explained through their influence alone.

In 1764 there appeared in Boston the celebrated pamphlet of James Otis upon *The Rights of the British Colonies.* In it was brought forward the idea that the political and civil rights of the English colonists in no way rested upon a grant from the crown; even Magna Charta, old as it might be, was not the beginning of all things. "A time may come when Parliament shall declare every American charter void; but the natural, inherent, and inseparable rights of the colonists as men and as citizens would remain, and, whatever became of charters, can never be abolished till the general conflagration." [4]

In this pamphlet definite limitations of the legislative power "which have been established by God and by Nature" are already enumerated in the form of the later bills of rights. As the center of the whole stood the principal occasion of strife between the

[4] Bancroft, IV, pp. 145, 146.

colonies and the mother-country, the right of taxation. That the levying of taxes or duties without the consent of the people or of representatives of the colonies was not indeed contrary to the laws of the country, but contrary to the eternal laws of liberty.[5] But these limitations were none other than those enumerated by Locke, which "the law of God and of Nature has set for every legislative power in every state and in every form of government".

But these propositions of Locke's are here found in a very radical transformation. They are changing namely from law to personal right. While Locke, similar to Rousseau later, places the individuals in subjection to the will of the majority of the community, upon which, however, restrictions are placed by the objects of the state, now the individual establishes the conditions under which he will enter the community, and in the state holds fast to these conditions as rights. He has accordingly rights in the state and claims upon the state which do not spring from the state. In opposition to England's attempt to restrict these rights,

[5] *Cf.* John Adams, *Works*, X, Boston, 1856, p. 293.

the idea formally to declare them and to defend them grew all the stronger.

This formulation was influenced by a work that was published anonymously at Oxford in 1754, in which for the first time "absolute rights" of the English are mentioned.[6] It originated from no less a person than Blackstone.[7] These rights of the individual were voiced in Blackstone's words for the first time in a Memorial to the legislature, which is given in an appendix to Otis's pamphlet.[8] On November 20, 1772, upon the motion of Samuel Adams a plan, which he had worked out, of a declaration of rights of the colonists as men, Christians and citizens was adopted by all the assembled citizens of Boston. It was therein declared, with an appeal to Locke, that men enter into the state by voluntary agreement, and they have the right beforehand in an equitable compact to establish conditions and limitations for the state and to see to it that these

---

[6] *Analysis of the Laws of England*, Chap. 4.

[7] It formed the basis of Blackstone's later *Commentaries*.

[8] *Cf.* Otis, *The Rights of the British Colonies asserted and proved*, 1764, reprinted London, p. 106.

are carried out. Thereupon the colonists demanded as men the right of liberty and of property, as Christians freedom of religion, and as citizens the rights of Magna Charta and of the Bill of Rights of 1689.[9]

Finally, on October 14, 1774, the Congress, representing twelve colonies, assembled in Philadelphia adopted a declaration of rights, according to which the inhabitants of the North American Colonies have rights which belong to them by the unchangeable law of nature, by the principles of the constitution of England and by their own constitutions.[10]

From that to the declaration of rights by Virginia is apparently only a step, and yet there is a world-wide difference between the two documents. The declaration of Philadelphia is a protest, that of Virginia a law. The appeal to England's law has disappeared. The state of Virginia solemnly recognizes rights pertaining to the present

[9] *Cf.* Wells, *The Life and Public Services of Samuel Adams*, I, Boston, 1865, pp. 502–507; Laboulaye, II, p. 171.

[10] The entire text reproduced in Story, *Commentaries on the Constitution of the United States*, 3d ed., I, pp. 134 *et seq.*

and future generations as the basis and foundation of government.[11]

In this and the following declarations of rights by the now sovereign states of North America, by the side of the rights of liberty that had been thus far asserted,—liberty of person, of property and of conscience,—stand new ones, corresponding to the infringements most recently suffered at England's hands of other lines of individual liberty: the right of assembly, the freedom of the press and free movement. But these rights of liberty were not the only ones therein asserted, there were the right of petition, the demand for the protection of law and the forms to be observed in insuring that, a special demand for trial by an independent jury, and in the same way with regard to other acts of the state; and the foundations of the citizen's political rights were also declared. They thus contained according to the intentions of their authors the distinctive features of the entire public

---

[11] The heading of the bill of rights reads: "A declaration of rights made by the representatives of the good people of Virginia, assembled in full and free convention; which rights do pertain to them and their posterity, as the basis and foundation of government."

right of the individual. Besides these were included the principle of the division of powers, of rotation of office, of accountability of office-holders, of forbidding hereditary titles, and there were further contained certain limitations on the legislature and executive, such as forbidding the keeping of a standing army or creating an established church,—all of which do not engender personal rights of the individual at all, or do so only indirectly. The whole is based upon the principle of the sovereignty of the people, and culminates in the conception of the entire constitution being an agreement of all concerned. In this particular one sees clearly the old Puritan-Independent idea of the covenant in its lasting influence, of which new power was to be significantly displayed later. When to-day in the separate states of the Union changes in the constitution are enacted either by the people themselves, or through a constitutional convention, there still lives in this democratic institution the same idea that once animated the settlers of Connecticut and Rhode Island.

Everywhere the bill of rights forms the first part of the constitution, following which as second part comes the plan or frame of government. The right of the creator of the state, the originally free and unrestricted individual, was first established, and then the right of that which the individuals created, namely, the community.

In spite of the general accord of these fundamental principles, when it came to carrying them out in practical legislation great differences arose in the various states, and though these differences were afterward greatly lessened they have not entirely disappeared even to-day. Thus, as mentioned above, religious liberty, in spite of its universal recognition in the constitutions, was not everywhere nor at once carried out in all of its consequences. In spite of the assertion that all men are by nature free and equal the abolition of slavery was not then accomplished. In the slave states in place of "man" stood "freeman".

The rights thus formally declared belonged originally to all the "inhabitants", in the slave states to all the "whites". It was only later that the qualification of citizenship of the United States was required in most of the states for the exercise of political rights.

We have thus seen by what a remarkable course of development there arose out of the

English law, old and new, that was practised in the colonies, the conception of a sphere of rights of the individual, which was independent of the state, and by the latter was simply to be recognized. In reality, however, the declarations of rights did nothing else than express the existing condition of rights in definite universal formulas.

That which the Americans already enjoyed they wished to proclaim as a perpetual possession for themselves and for every free people. In contrast to them the French wished to give that which they did not yet have, namely, institutions to correspond to their universal principles. Therein lies the most significant difference between the American and French declarations of rights, that in the one case the institutions preceded the recognition of rights of the individual, in the other they followed after. Therein lay also the fatal mistake of the German National Assembly at Frankfort which wished to determine first the rights of the individual and then establish the state. The German state was not yet founded, but it was already settled what this state not yet existing dare not do and what it had to concede. The Americans could calmly precede their plan of government with a bill of rights, because that government and the controlling laws had already long existed.

One thing, however, has resulted from this investigation with irrefutable certainty. The principles of 1789 are in reality the principles of 1776.

CHAPTER IX.

THE RIGHTS OF MAN AND THE TEUTONIC CONCEPTION OF RIGHT.

IN conclusion there remains still one question to answer. Why is it that the doctrine of an original right of the individual and of a state compact, arising as far back as the time of the Sophists in the ancient world, further developed in the mediæval theory of Natural Law, and carried on by the currents of the Reformation,—why is it that this doctrine advanced to epoch-making importance for the first time in England and her colonies? And in general, in a thoroughly monarchical state, all of whose institutions are inwardly bound up with royalty and only through royalty can be fully comprehended, how could republican ideas press in and change the structure of the state so completely?

The immediate cause thereof lies clearly before us. The antagonism between the dynasty of the Stuarts, who came from a foreign land and relied upon their divine right, and the English national conceptions of right, and also the religious wars with royalty in England and Scotland, seem to have sufficiently favored the spreading of doctrines which were able to arouse an energetic opposition. Yet similar conditions existed in many a Continental state from the end of the sixteenth to the middle of the seventeenth century. There, too, arose a strong opposition of the estates to royalty which was striving more and more towards absolutism, fearful religious wars broke out and an extensive literature sought with great energy to establish rights of the people and of the individual over against the rulers. The revolutionary ideas on the continent led it is true in France to regicide, but there was nowhere an attempt made at a reconstruction of the whole state system. Locke's doctrines of a Law of Nature appear to have had no influence at all outside of England. The Continental doctrines of natural law played their important part for the first time at the end of the eighteenth century in the great social transformation of the French Revolution.

It was not without result that England in distinction from the Continent had withstood the influence of the Roman Law. The English legal conceptions have by no means remained untouched by the Roman, but they have not been nearly so deeply influenced by them as the Continental. The public law especially developed upon an essentially Teutonic basis, and the original Teutonic ideas of right have never been overgrown with the later Roman conceptions of the state's omnipotence.

The Teutonic state, however, in distinction from the ancient, so far as the latter is historically known to us, rose from weak beginnings to increasing power. The competence of the Teutonic state was in the beginning very narrow, the individual was greatly restricted by his family and clan, but not by the state. The political life of the Middle Ages found expression rather in associations than in a state which exhibited at first only rudimentary forms.

At the beginning of modern times the power of the state became more and more concentrated. This could happen in England all the easier because the Norman kings had already strongly centralized the administration. As early as the end of the sixteenth century Sir Thomas Smith could speak of the unrestricted power of the English Parliament,[1] which Coke a little later declared to be "absolute and transcendent".[2]

But this power was thought of by Englishmen as unlimited only in a nominal legal sense. That the state, and therefore Parliament and the King have very real restrictions placed upon them has been at all times in England a live conviction of the people.

Magna Charta declares that the liberties and rights conceded by it are granted "*in perpetuum*".[3] In the Bill of Rights it was ordained that everything therein contained should "remain the law of this realm for-

---

[1] "The most high and absolute power of the realm of England consisteth in the Parliament . . . all that ever the people of Rome might do, either in *centuriatis comitiis* or *tributis*, the same may be done by the Parliament of England, which representeth and hath the power of the whole realm, both the head and the body." *The Commonwealth of England*, 1589, Book II, reprinted in Prothero, *Select Statutes and Documents of Elizabeth and James I.*, Oxford, 1894, p. 178.

[2] 4 *Inst.* p. 36.

[3] Art. 63. Stubbs, p. 306.

ever ".[4] In spite of the nominal omnipotence of the state a limit which it shall not overstep is specifically demanded and recognized in the most important fundamental laws.

In these nominally legal but perfectly meaningless stipulations, the old Teutonic legal conception of the state's limited sphere of activity finds expression.

The movement of the Reformation was also based on the idea of the restriction of the state. Here, however, there entered the conception of a second restriction which was conditioned by the entire historical development. The mediæval state found restrictions not only in the strength of its members, but also in the sphere of the church. The question as to how far the state's right extended in spiritual matters could only be fully raised after the Reformation, because through the Reformation those limits which had been fixed in the Middle Ages again became disputable. The new defining of the religious sphere and the withdrawal of the state from that sphere were also on the lines of necessary historical development.

So the conception of the superiority of the

[4] Art. 11. Stubbs, p. 527.

individual over against the state found its support in the entire historical condition of England in the seventeenth century. The doctrines of a natural law attached themselves to the old conceptions of right, which had never died, and brought them out in new form.

The same is true of the theories that arose on the Continent. Since the predominance of the historical school, one is accustomed to look upon the doctrines of a natural law as impossible dreaming. But an important fact is thereby overlooked, that no theory, no matter how abstract it may seem, which wins influence upon its time can do so entirely outside of the field of historical reality.

An insight into these historical facts is of the greatest importance for a correct legal comprehension of the relation of the state and the individual. There are here two possibilities, both of which can be logically carried out. According to the one the entire sphere of right of the individual is the product of state concession and permission. According to the other the state not only engenders rights of the individual, but it also leaves the individual that measure of liberty which it does not itself require in the interest of the whole. This liberty, however, it does not create but only recognizes.

The first conception is based upon the idea of the state's omnipotence as it was most sharply defined in the absolutist doctrines of the sixteenth and seventeenth centuries. Its extreme consequence has been drawn by the poet in his question of law:

"Jahrelang schon bedien' ich mich meiner Nase
　　zum Riechen;
Hab' ich denn wirklich an sie auch ein erweis-
　　liches Recht?"[5]

The second theory on the other hand is that of the Teutonic conception of right corresponding to the historical facts of the gradual development of the state's power. If natural right is identical with non-historical right, then the first doctrine is for the modern state that of natural right, the second that of historical right. However much the boundaries of that recognized liberty have changed in the course of time, the consciousness that such boundaries existed was never

[5] For years I have used my nose to smell with,
Have I then really a provable right to it?

extinguished in the Teutonic peoples even at the time of the absolute state.[6]

This liberty accordingly was not created but recognized, and recognized in the self-limitation of the state and in thus defining the intervening spaces which must necessarily remain between those rules with which the state surrounds the individual. What thus remains is not so much a right as it is a condition. The great error in the theory of a natural right lay in conceiving of the actual condition of liberty as a right and ascribing

---

[6] The idea of all individual rights of liberty being the product of state concession has been recently advocated by Tezner, *Grünhuts Zeitschrift für Privat- und öffentliches Recht*, XXI, pp. 136 *et seq.*, who seeks to banish the opposing conception to the realm of natural right. The decision of such important questions can only be accomplished by careful historical analysis, which will show different results for different epochs,— that, for example, the legal nature of liberty is entirely different in the ancient state and in the modern. Legal dialectics can easily deduce the given condition with equally logical acuteness from principles directly opposed to one another. The true principle is taught not by jurisprudence but by history.

to this right a higher power which creates and restricts the state.[7]

At first glance the question does not seem to be of great practical significance, whether an act of the individual is one directly permitted by the state or one only indirectly recognized. But it is not the task of the science of law merely to train the judge and the administrative officer and teach them to decide difficult cases. To recognize the true boundaries between the individual and the community is the highest problem that thoughtful consideration of human society has to solve.

[7] *Cf.* more explicitly on this, Jellinek, *loc. cit.,* pp. 43, 89 *et seq.*

SECOND IMPRESSION.

FORD'S THE FEDERALIST.

Edited by PAUL LEICESTER FORD, editor of the writings of Jefferson; Bibliography of the Constitution of the United States, 1787-1788; Pamphlets on the Constitution of the United States. lxxvii + 793 pp. Large 12mo. $1.75, *net.*

The present edition is the first in which any attempt has been made to illustrate, in foot-notes, not merely the obscure passages in the text, but also the subsequent experience of the United States and other countries where they relate to the views expressed by the authors. The most authentic text has been used; the antiquated and often absurd punctuation—largely due to incompetent early printers—has been rationalized; and an introduction, abundant cross-references, and a *full index* materially increase the value of this edition for both students and lawyers. Matter of obsolete or minor interest has been put in distinctive type. An appendix of 149 pages contains The Constitution with all the amendments, and the references to U. S. Reports, besides other documents important in constitutional developement.

Roger Foster, author of Commentaries on the Constitution: "The best edition of *The Federalist* that has been published."

Right Hon. James Bryce: "Far the best [edition] I have seen, and the most likely to be useful to students of political science."

New York Tribune: "Mr. Ford's editing is nothing less than perfect. ... Printed handsomely and published in a convenient size, this is an invaluable edition, calculated to be of service not only to the politician and lawyer, but to every thoughtful citizen."

Review of Reviews: "Mr. Ford has the habit of thoroughness in a very remarkable degree; ... not only great ability, but rare opportunities and invaluable experience.... A soundly edited text; ... an introductory essay which really puts the touch of finality upon questions that have been in dispute for nearly a century.... For the purposes of critical study and precise reference Mr. Ford's edition, it seems to us, must of necessity exclude all others. Quite apart from the extremely valuable editorial work included in the introductory part of the volume, Mr. Ford's index (*The Federalist* has never before been indexed) would entitle him to a vote of thanks by Congress."

Prof. Edward G. Bourne, of Yale: "The most useful edition for the working student."

The Dial: "Mr. Paul Leicester Ford has many titles to the gratitude of students interested in American history, and none more clear than that which is due him for his edition of *The Federalist.* ... The work is admirably done in all important respects, and should be upon the desk of every teacher of American constitutional history."

Prof. Carl Evans Boyd, of University of Chicago: "His edition leaves nothing to be desired, and will undoubtedly become the standard."

The Outlook: "A singularly illuminative introduction; ... one of the best planned and most valuable contributions ever made towards the clearer understanding of our history."

HENRY HOLT & CO., 29 West 23d Street, New York.

GORDY'S POLITICAL PARTIES IN THE UNITED STATES Vol. I, 1783-1809. 598 pp. 12mo. $1.75, *net, special.*

A work intended for the thoughtful reader without much previous knowledge of the subject. To be completed in four volumes, the second of which is now in press.

Nation: "Four years ago we had an opportunity to pronounce a favorable judgment on it. . . . Now there is much extension in addition to a thorough revision. . . . The opening sentences (no mean criterion often) are of a nature to whet the appetite for what is to come."

LEE'S SOURCE BOOK OF ENGLISH HISTORY

Edited by Dr. GUY CARLTON LEE. 609 pp. 12mo. $2.00, *net.*

Some 200 documents and selections from contemporaries from Herodotus to the last treaty with the Boers. With a full Bibliography of Sources (60 pp.).

N. Y. Tribune: "The generous scope of the work would alone commend it to the student. *Every detail in the book increases his gratitude.* . . . Mr. Lee appears to have used the best judgment, choosing just such documents as the reader desires to get at. . . . Altogether, this is a most serviceable publication. Mr. Lee's little introductory notes to his various documents are judiciously brief, but always sufficient and interesting."

HENDERSON'S SIDE LIGHTS ON ENGLISH HISTORY

With 80 full-page illustrations. 300 pp. 8vo. $5.00, *net special.*

Accounts and pictures by contemporaries ingeniously arranged to give the effect of a continuous history, and dealing with such topics as the personality of Queen Elizabeth, the execution of Mary Stuart, characteristic traits of Cromwell, the return of Charles II., the Stuarts in exile, Queen Anne and the Marlboroughs, etc., etc., illustrated by 80 portraits, fac-similes, caricatures, etc., reproduced directly from the rarest original mezzotint and line engravings.

N. Y. Tribune: "It is not unlikely that he who has dipped into this book in the early afternoon will find himself still reading when night comes. . . . **A better book to put in the hands of the lover of history, whether he be a beginner or an old student, we do not know.**"

WALKER'S DISCUSSIONS IN ECONOMICS AND STATISTICS

By the late General FRANCIS A. WALKER. Edited by Prof. DAVIS R. DEWEY.

With portrait. 454 + 481 pp. 2 vols. 8vo. $6.00, *net special.*

The Dial: "Clear and interesting to the general reader, as well as instructive to the careful student."

BRÉAL'S SEMANTICS lxvi + 336 pp. 12mo, $2.50, *net.*

Studies in the Science of Significations, as distinguished from the Science of Sounds (Phonetics). The style is pleasing, and the enjoyment of the book requires no previous philological training.

SWEET'S PRACTICAL STUDY OF LANGUAGES

By Prof. HENRY SWEET of Oxford. 12mo. $1.50, *net.*

"Clear and interesting to the general reader, as well as instructive to the careful student."—*The Dial.*

AN IMPORTANT WORK BY THE LATE

FRANCIS A. WALKER

President of the Massachusetts Institute of Technology; Professor of Political Economy and History in Sheffield Scientific School of Yale College; late chief of the U. S. Bureau of Statistics; Superintendent of the Ninth Census; author of the Statistical Atlas of the United States, etc.

DISCUSSIONS IN ECONOMICS AND STATISTICS

Edited by Professor DAVIS R. DEWEY.
With portrait.   454 + 481 pp.   2 vols.   8vo. $6.00, *net.*

VOL. I. **Finance and Taxation, Money and Bimetallism, Economic Theory.**
VOL. II. **Statistics, National Growth, Social Economics.**

The author had hoped to bring these papers together himself.

The Dial: "Professor Dewey has performed a real service to the public, as well as to the memory of his late chief. . . . In the present collection the editor has not included everything General Walker ever wrote, but has aimed, so far as possible, to avoid repetitions of thought. . . there are some discussions of the national finances in the period following the Civil War, which have a timely as well as historical interest at the present time. . . . To improve the census was General Walker's work for many years, and his experience cannot fail to be of interest to the present generation. . . . Economics in the hands of this master was no dismal science, because of his broad sympathies, his healthy conservative optimism, his belief in the efficacy of effort ; and, in a more superficial sense, because of his saving sense of humor and his happy way of putting things, . . . he was the fortunate possessor of a very pleasing literary style, . . . clear and interesting to the general reader, as well as instructive to the careful student."

The Outlook: "This book makes accessible for students the miscellaneous work of one of America's greatest political economists. . . . Dr. Dewey has performed his critical work with the reverence of a disciple, and reprinted in full all the more important contributions."

Political Science Quarterly: "The collection embraces between fifty and sixty articles, all of them characterized by the forceful reasoning and balanced judgment of the gifted author."

HENRY HOLT & CO.   29 W. 23d St., NEW YORK
378 Wabash Ave., CHICAGO

"A fitting memorial to its author."—*The Dial*

A NOTABLE BOOK BY THE LATE

FRANCIS A. WALKER
President of the Massachusetts Institute of Technology

DISCUSSIONS IN EDUCATION

Edited by JAMES PHINNEY MUNROE. 8vo. $3.00, *net.*

The author had hoped himself to collect these papers in a volume. They are grouped under *Technological Education, Manual Education, The Teaching of Arithmetic* and *College Problems* (including *College Athletics*). *A Valedictory* appropriately closes the book.

The Outlook: "Space fails us here to transcribe some passages we had marked as maxims for the times. So long as the reforms and improvements in our educational methods which General Walker advocated, not without some success, are but partially accomplished, will this volume of expert testimony deserve to be close at hand to those with whom is the responsibility of direction."

The Dial: "A fitting memorial to its author. . . The breadth of his experience, as well as the natural range of his mind, are here reflected. The subjects dealt with are all live and practical. . . . He never deals with them in a narrow or so-called 'practical' way."

The Boston Transcript: "Two of his conspicuous merits characterize these papers, the peculiar power he possessed of enlisting and retaining the attention for what are commonly supposed to be dry and difficult subjects, and the capacity he had for controversy, sharp and incisive, but so candid and generous that it left no festering wound."

The Review of Reviews: "A strong presentation of the scope and dignity of technological education, and its relations to other forms of culture."

The School Review: "The scope and power of the contents make the work a permanent contribution to the development of educational thought and principle."

EARLIER BOOKS BY GEN. FRANCIS A. WALKER

(*Circular free.*) *Wages.* 428 pp. 12mo. $2.00.—*Money.* 550 pp. 12mo. $2.00.—*Money in its Relations to Trade and Industry.* 339 pp. 12mo. $1.25.—*International Bimetallism.* 297 pp. 12mo. $1.25.—*Political Economy (Advanced Course.* 537 pp. 8vo. $2.00, *net.*—*Briefer Course.* 415 pp. 12mo. $1.20, *net.*—*Elementary Course.* 323 pp. 12mo. $1.00, *net.*)

HENRY HOLT & CO.   29 West 23d St., NEW YORK
378 Wabash Ave., CHICAGO

2d Impression of
THE FORTUNE OF WAR

By Miss ELIZABETH BARROW. 12mo. $1.25.

A vivid romance, the scene of which is laid in New York City during the British Occupation in the Revolution.

N. Y. Times Saturday Review: "The story is a good one, the historical data accurate, and the ways and manners of the period are cleverly presented. . . . **The love plot is absorbing, and will be found by many readers even more fascinating than the faithful reproduction of the manners and customs of the time. . . . It is quite safe to say that this book vies in excellence with some of the historical romances which have caused more general comment. No doubt it will gradually grow into a larger popularity.**

The Outlook: "Miss Elizabeth Barrow has done her work not only well, but delightfully well."

The Independent: "A short tale, and a very good one. . . . A story of the Revolutionary War, romantic to a degree and very charmingly told."

Chicago Times-Herald: "Another tale of the time of Washington, but one that is more deserving both of popular and critical appreciation than some of the much-vaunted financial successes."

Springfield Republican: "It gives a good picture of New York City as it was in the eighteenth century. . . . The story is agreeable reading."

Hartford Courant: "She has done good work in her romance; . . . it is told in a very attractive way. . . . The book is decidedly one that will entertain."

Christian Register: "Miss Barrow has been successful in depicting the condition of New York City at the time the British were quartered there. . . It is a bright, pleasant tale."

The Churchman: "The book furnishes an interesting sidelight upon the estimation in which the Americans were held by the upper classes of the British through the greater part of the Revolutionary struggle."

HENRY HOLT & CO.   29 West 23d Street
New York

RUSSIA

KRAUSSE'S RUSSIA IN ASIA, 1558–1899

With appendix, index, and twelve maps. 8vo. $4.00.

Boston Transcript: "The most masterly marshaling of the British arguments against Russia which has appeared in a long time. . . . The man who wrote the book has had an inside view of Russian methods, or else he is extremely clever in collecting detailed information about them. His information is brought down to date, and his passages on the Manchurian railway agreement show that he can see near things as vividly as far things. His review of the present state of Russia's southern boundary in Asia is striking, and sums up a great deal of history."

THOMPSON'S RUSSIAN POLITICS

By Herbert M. Thompson. An account of the relations of Russian geography, history, and politics, and of the bearings of the last on questions of world-wide interest. With maps. 12mo. $2.00.

Outlook: "The result of careful study, compactly, clearly, and effectively presented. . . . The author's aim is to stir the friends of freedom throughout the world to a deeper interest in the cause of Russian liberty. His work is vivified by the fact that his heart is in it."

WALLACE'S RUSSIA

By D. Mackenzie Wallace, M. A., Member of the Imperial Russian Geographical Society. Large 12mo. $2.00.

Contents include: In the Northern Forests; Voluntary Exile; The Village Priest; A Peasant Family of the Old Type; The Mir, or Village Community; Towns and Mercantile Classes; Lord Novgorod the Great; The Imperial Administration; The New Local Self-Government; Proprietors of the Modern School; The Noblesse; Social Classes; Among the Heretics; Pastoral Tribes of the Steppes: St. Petersburg and European Influence; Church and State; The Crimean War and Its Consequences; The Serfs; The New Law Courts; Territorial Expansion and the Eastern Question.

Nation: "Worthy of the highest praise. . . . Not a piece of clever book-making, but the result of a large amount of serious study and thorough research. . . . We commend his book as a very valuable account of a very interesting people."

GAUTIER'S A WINTER IN RUSSIA

By Théophile Gautier. Translated by M. M. Ripley. 12mo. $1.75.

Contents: Berlin; Hamburg; Schleswig; Lübeck; Crossing the Baltic; St. Petersburg; Winter; The Neva; Details of Interiors; A Ball at the Winter Palace; The Theatres; The Tchoukine Dvor; Zichy; St. Isaac's; Moscow; The Kremlin; Troïtza; Byzantine Art; Return to France.

New York Tribune: "As little like an ordinary book of travel as a slender antique vase filled with the perfumed wine of Horatian banquets is like the fat comfortable tea-cup of a modern breakfast-table."

HENRY HOLT & CO. 29 West 23d Street New York

CPSIA information can be obtained
at www.ICGtesting.com
Printed in the USA
BVHW012141170422
634574BV00002B/15